T0207626

THE WISDOM OF DEATH

Insights to Living Life Fully

ESHA ESTAR

Copyright © 2021 Esha Estar.

All rights reserved. No part of this book may be used or reproduced by any means, graphic, electronic, or mechanical, including photocopying, recording, taping or by any information storage retrieval system without the written permission of the author except in the case of brief quotations embodied in critical articles and reviews.

Balboa Press books may be ordered through booksellers or by contacting:

Balboa Press
A Division of Hay House
1663 Liberty Drive
Bloomington, IN 47403
www.balboapress.com
844-682-1282

Because of the dynamic nature of the Internet, any web addresses or links contained in this book may have changed since publication and may no longer be valid. The views expressed in this work are solely those of the author and do not necessarily reflect the views of the publisher, and the publisher hereby disclaims any responsibility for them.

Any people depicted in stock imagery provided by Getty Images are models, and such images are being used for illustrative purposes only. Certain stock imagery © Getty Images.

ISBN: 978-1-9822-5793-4 (sc)
ISBN: 978-1-9822-5792-7 (e)

Library of Congress Control Number: 2020921562

Print information available on the last page.

Balboa Press rev. date: 01/27/2021

ESHA ESTAR

Grief Shaman

Join our community!

We believe that humanity is ready to reframe their grief stories to courageously step into a new paradigm shift of hope, compassion, and heart resiliency. We aim to create meaningful connections that both are non-judgmental and inspiring as we learn to view our grief stories through the lens of liberation.

As a Grief Shaman, my mission is to be a guide to humanity in reframing our grief stories, moving from suffering to liberation.

GO TO WWW.ESHAESTAR.COM TO FIND MANY MORE RESOURCES FOR YOUR JOURNEY INCLUDING...

Online Social Community - Stories of Liberation from Suffering – Facebook and Instagram (@eshaestar)
One on One with Esha (Mariposa: A Grief Sanctuary)
Workbooks on Grief, End of Life Planning, Contemplative Journals
Books
Speaking Engagements
Group Retreats (Coming in 2021)
Mobile App (Coming in 2021)
Online Courses and Teacher Trainings (Coming in 2021)

To the courageous hearts of all those who have lost
loved ones and dare to love and live fully.

Death was like an unfamiliar friend watching from a distance.
Like a far-off examiner, she stood watching, observing,
assessing me. Her silent stare was making me uncomfortable in my skin.
I wanted to look away but could not.
There was not a smile, a smirk, or a sympathetic gaze.
Her face ever watchful, waiting, but for what? Then one day I happened to
notice she no longer stood as a distant unfamiliar friend.
Somehow when I wasn't looking, death had sauntered up
to me, holding my hand reassuringly.
I stood confused at this intrusion until I realized that
my beloved was no more, and death had come to pay me
a close visit.
Still, she didn't smile, she didn't smirk; she simply held my
hand. I tossed her hand away and began to yell and scream
at her presence, but she persisted.
Everything within me rebelled, wanted to deny. But the look
in death's eyes assured me that if I stayed and was present
with the pain and fear of my loss, I would find my way
through this unexpected grief.
Death stayed with me through the yelling and crying, like an
old friend who knew the pain, the heartache of loss.
She stood with me, refusing to leave my side, holding my hand
until my breath slowed, till the freshness of each inhale smelled
like something I could remember.
She stayed till I could accept.
Accept the moment of endings and beginnings.
So we stood, death holding my hand as my beloved transitioned.
We stood side by side, quietly present.
Accepting. Death.

THE WISDOM OF DEATH

On August 2, 2017, I unexpectedly lost my husband to a pulmonary embolism that killed him on his way home at an airport in the Caribbean with our two teenage daughters present to witness it. He was forty-five and in the best shape of his life. Ironically, I had just returned home from a death and dying workshop in Thailand. We were married for twenty years, and his sudden departure dropped me into a dark space, where I went into an existential crisis and began to contemplate the nature of death. Two years before his death, I lost my mother to diabetic complications. This book is my journey with death and dying and the wisdom death may have for each of us to step into living life with fullness.

Through much of my grief, death was a sitting companion that dared me to be still. It stripped me to the core, and I hated it. For weeks and months, I prayed for death to leave; I had had enough. This unexpected loss left me feeling confused, angry, resentful, and exhausted. Initially, fear gripped me, and I kept thinking, *I am next.* I fell into a space of wanting to be here and not here. The here part still had so much left to do, children to be around for, a life left to live, and yet the lure of leaving it all behind was freeing.

As the months sped by, I got tired of fighting with death, tired of holding the fear, tired of loss, and tired of the constant anxiety. With nothing left to do but surrender, I decided to open myself to receiving the lessons death had to offer.

I began to befriend death to see what it had to offer me, to listen to its sobering messages that were life altering. As I began to do that, I found that death had a lot to say. And as I listened and meditated on it daily, I thought that either I was crazy or something extraordinary was taking place. One of the first things that happened to me after I gave myself permission to embrace death and her teachings was my fears and anxieties began to subside considerably. I began to give myself permission to be with death, to let go and open my heart and soul in a much bigger way than I had ever done before. I became more loving to myself, more forgiving, more compassionate, and more peaceful. Death was showing me how to show up to this life fully to be more authentic and to live. Death gives us a rare view of how small we are playing in this life. It also shows us the rearview mirror of life passing by when we fail to let go of the smallness we have become so accustomed to being.

My time meditating on death and seeing myself in a coffin, however morbid that may sound, humbled me beyond words. I saw my own beautiful innocence, felt the deepest compassion and love, and realized that what death was really showing me was how to give all of myself to the dance of life. It is my hope that we will all learn how to dance and embrace this life with an inner spark that gives us courage to sparkle.

I admit I fell into this death and dying thing by accident years before my mother and husband died, but they say nothing is an accident. Regardless of how I have arrived here, I am here, and my desire is simply to bring awareness to something we can't really understand. Perhaps we can courageously share our feelings, thoughts, and desires for our own endings in this physical skin.

I don't write this from a place of absolute fearlessness. I am still afraid. How will I die? What will happen to my children? When will it happen? The questions are many, and there are no answers coming. I must wait just like everyone else till that moment is revealed and trust that I've done what I was put on this good earth to do, that I dared to love so much, and that I didn't leave anything behind.

Death has revealed to me to be fully present in this body right now. It allows me to keep letting go so more space is made for the next experience. Death is the master teacher of all teachers that ironically teaches you how to live fully now. Yes, we must plan and put things in order, but we must live for life. Death then can point us in the direction of intentional living, to honor every moment as if they all belong. Death has reminded me not to put off my happiness and joy for some far-off moment when things will get better but instead to embrace joy now.

This book is not written to teach you how to die or give you tips on the nature of life after death. Rather, it serves to teach you how to live through the eyes and lenses of death. We do not have to wait to be on our deathbeds to find gratitude. We can make our daily lives our deathbeds and take everything we feel to guide us into the lives we dare to live fully. We can stare at our regrets and turn them into dreams actualized. Our daily deathbeds can help us to find our authentic selves and courageously bring them to life. It redirects and reorders life. It frees us from stagnation and reminds us that now is the time. It frees us from our small "I" self and puts us in touch with our true selves. It frees us from a *should* mentality to a *could* mentality. Finally, it moves us from worthlessness to worthiness. For in death we are all equals. There is no hierarchy, no superior race, no gender, and no caste system. The numbers in our bank accounts are zeroed out as we returned to that zero space of being. In death we are true brothers and sisters of the same cloth, spiritual beings occupying a human experience, as Pierre Teilhard de Chardin so eloquently quoted.

I hope this book inspires you to live your best life as it has surely inspired me to live mine. Perhaps it will also embolden you to reach for the impossible in your life and reach for those long-forgotten dreams of your childhood. Maybe, just maybe it sparks enough interest to begin the conversations in your home or small circle of friends. Maybe instead of having book clubs where we talk about books, we can start death clubs where we get together to share our honest feelings on the topic. I see this discussion as a way for us to get involved so our human race can evolve and embrace all our humanity, not just parts of it. Thank you for reading this reflective book on death. I hope it inspires and gives birth to something wonderful inside you as you step fully into the life you're meant to live.

Blessings to your joy!

WHAT IS DEATH?

What is death? The question itself is so enormous that the answer is a mystery. We have only received glimpses through near-death experiences, and books such as the *Tibetan Book of the Dead* give us some insights. But we do not *really* know. So, as I write this book, I cannot claim to know or give you an answer on what death truly is. It is above my pay grade, and I do not have the clearance for that.

What we do know is the clinical version of death. Death, according to Merriam-Webster definition, is the cessation of all vital functions. This is but one part of the whole story. Where the spirit goes after death is mystery for us to hold in awe.

As stated previously, there are many books written on life after death, heaven, near-death experiences, and so much more. This book is not one of them. I cannot profess to know what exists after life because I am still here on this earth plane. So, I focus on how death can teach us how to live as a transformative agent for the greater good.

We are all fragile in these human bodies, dressed in borrowed skin that will have to be returned to the shop maker. This skin over time becomes weathered and seasoned with years of experiences adorning its inner and outer surfaces. Some of us take great care of it, and others abuse it. Yet there is no judgment, only experiences. We cannot take the adornments with us. Those we must leave here for others to talk and reminisce about over a good glass of ale.

This innocent vulnerability we hold reminds us that we are chipped, broken, whole, and complete at the same time. Death keeps reminding us of this fragility, the soft place within us we don't want to recognize or admit to. We are constantly being asked, "Where are the rigid places inside us we have hidden?" The hard is the place we want to hold on to for dear life. It is the safe and comfortable that has grown like barnacles in the interior self. Yet I find it is in the soft and uncomfortable place that life beckons us to come alive. This tender place is the part that feels the crucible of life's pains and joys, and we have the courage, even with trembling legs, to witness our unfolding.

Similarly, we come to our deathbeds with a trembling of the unknown. We are afraid of the shadows that lurk in the dark between the veil of this life and the next. Yet if we have the audacity to accept the soft tender place within us, we approach that trembling with more curiosity. We can do this because we have developed a bold kind of trust that whatever is on the other side is another adventure waiting to be lived and living our lives in the soft prepares us for that.

The soft is the path of vulnerability that gives us an inner strength to express a compassionate humanity. This compassion for our humanity helps us to let go of resentment, victimization, anger, shame, guilt, unworthiness, and love. These experiences, if we can see them as such, are all preparation for dying to what is, which is always the moment that has passed. Death is constantly on the horizon, supporting us in a mysterious way to let go and move on to the next adventure and life. With such a viewpoint, we can know that victory is with us always; we shed one moment, one breath, one life for the next. Yet most of society is not ready to accept death or the sacred teachings it may offer. Death is still a taboo, elephant-in-the-room topic that prevents us from being in relationship with it. What can we hope to learn from this teacher?

Being in relationship with death takes us to this tender place, where we come face-to-face with our own reflections and seize the opportunity to befriend the stranger we have become to ourselves. When a loved one passes, it forces us to come to grips with our own mortality, the effects of loneliness, our finiteness, and the unshakable acceptance that death is the one part of our stories that has already been written out for us. Mortality suddenly stares us in the face when death comes close to us. We hope that we can arrive at the door of death without regrets and with peace, a life lived fully, and integrity. We surrender this life knowing we lived it bravely, we employed compassion and zest for the journey, and we realize that every step along our existence is a learning experience toward more love.

It is interesting how the attitude surrounding death and dying has changed over the last hundred years or so. We went from a culture that kept our dead in the home for three days to only having a few minutes, if that much, before sending them off to the funeral home. By sitting with our dying loved ones before and after, we receive the gifts of courage, compassion, forgiveness, peace, and love as we look death square in the face to see and honor our own mortality.

We no longer sit sacredly with our loved one's body and make peace with his or her passing and our being left alone. It is a quick series of letting go without honoring in an intentional way the nature of death and our grief. I don't have anything against funeral parlors; they serve a purpose for sure. But we have become a nation that is unused to being with death, either talking about it or simply sitting with a loved one's body. Like our very fast-paced culture, the death process seems to have a drive-through lane. Put in your order at the window and be on your way as quickly as possible. We are losing a vital part of our humanity by bypassing our emotions, fears, anxieties, to hurry back to a state of "normal" busyness. Our resistance to making peace with mortality only lends to our heightened fears surrounding death. We do not talk about death with each other and our children, and when it comes, there is shock. We are all surprised when it arrives to our shores, and we are all ill prepared.

Instead of denying that each of us is not here in this physical body forever, let us talk about what death can truly reveal to us. How it can help us to live a fuller life by keeping it a constant in our lives. How it can help us plan financially, leave a will, life insurance, detailed instructions about what we want and don't want at our funerals. How can it help us to become softer, more loving, and compassionate to ourselves and others? How can it help us to fulfill our destinies in this human skin to show up fully alive?

Even for those who wield power, life is brief.
There is only one way to triumph over death,
And this is by making our lives a masterpiece.
We must seize every opportunity to show
Kindness and to love fully.

—From *Origins* by Dan Brown

ESHA ESTAR

Grief Shaman

What does death ask of you? Be still.

Why are you running away from being with me? Why do I scare
you so? Come take a closer look, and tell me what you see.

Death is not the enemy. Rather, it is your fear of never accomplishing
your true desires and dreams that you let linger into regrets.

ESHA ESTAR

Grief Shaman

You are never forsaken for in life and in death, you are not alone.
In life, God is with you, and in death, God is with you. It all then
depends on what you believe. And even then, you are not alone.

Why are you so afraid of taking time to ponder me?

What comes up when you are faced with death?
What business are you not finished with?

I am not here to scare you. I am here to liberate you.

ESHA ESTAR

Grief Shaman

Keep me as a companion in your daily life,
and I will teach you how to be free.

Your true death is when you decide to bury your hopes,
dreams, desires, and who you really are out of fear.

Do not believe the old sayings they have taught you to believe.
I am not the Grim Reaper. I am the reaper of a new life.

Cast your net not on death but on your own limited views and version of
who you are. That is what truly holds you captive in your mental grave.

ESHA ESTAR

Grief Shaman

You are used to running away from me. I understand you are afraid, unable to see your own shadows within me. Yet I come not to hold you in the dark but to free you into the light.

I have been wrongly accused.

Do not be afraid of my face; it is the supreme wisdom of all life.

My job is not to coddle you into believing fairy tales about life. My job is lifting you out of darkness into resurrected life.

ESHA ESTAR

Grief Shaman

Why worry about the afterlife when life is
upon you now. "Live," I say. "Live."

If you would only sit with me and lean into my teachings,
you would know that I am not the bearer of bad news.

Come see what I have to offer, and then make up
your own mind on the nature of all things.

The world teaches you how to live for material things. Come
let me teach you how to live for love and true life.

ESHA ESTAR

Grief Shaman

You wander around each day feeling lost, angry,
depressed, unloved. Where is the life in that?

Do not wait till the end to wish upon a star. Your time is now.

What lies beyond death is not the end but a new beginning.

Don't be afraid of me. I come to reorient your
life to teach you how to live fully.

Everything in nature must die and be reborn. Why
then do you presume you are so different?

ESHA ESTAR

Grief Shaman

There is no ego in death. It falls away in the end to reveal who you truly are—a spirit encased in a human body experiencing love in a finite skin.

If you can practice death every day, you will know the joys of living.
Death teaches you that it is not all about you.
It is about service to each other.

Death accepts you exactly as you are.

There is tenderness on the deathbed, a reaching toward a deep need to embrace love. Love is the milk you seek. In the end, we come to see this.

ESHA ESTAR

Grief Shaman

Death does not judge; there is never a hung jury. All are walked
to this place regardless of color, creed, gender, political affiliation,
religious views. How wonderful to find something that is not biased.

You notice when you spend more time with me that you begin to dissolve,
the "small I" within yourself is let loose. What a wonderful liberation.

Stillness. Stillness. That is where you will find me.

Some of you are afraid to live, and some are afraid
to die. Where does that leave you?

ESHA ESTAR

Grief Shaman

When you are there, in that in-between place, you feel the tremble of your waning breath and the pull of the call to come home. You can let go into the arms of the ancestors waiting in jubilant celebration as they welcome you home with joy. You are never alone.

May I ask why you are not living fully? When will your living begin? How many more excuses shall stand in front of you and this very life you have?

It is interesting how you behave when you are alive. Griping about this and that. Gossiping about this or that. Angry about right and wrong, being a Democrat or Republican, rich, poor, black, white. Tell me, where are all those things when you are on your deathbed?

ESHA ESTAR

Grief Shaman

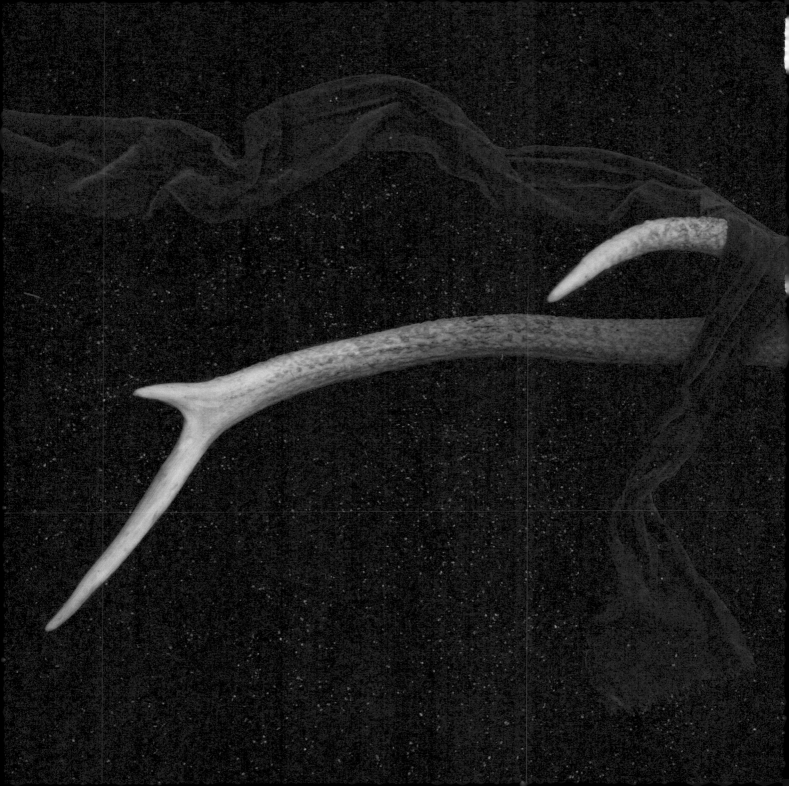

Isn't it funny that on the deathbed you don't want to be alone? Then remember to treat each other well in life.

In the end it is love that you desire. Only love.

Your light and your dark are welcome here.

I am an equal opportunity employer.

Kings, queens, presidents, dictators—all leaders come unto me in the end. You cannot wield your power here.

ESHA ESTAR

Grief Shaman

I am here to remind you to live.

You worry so much about whether you are living this life right that you forget to live. Life is not a contest about who gets the biggest trophy in the afterlife. Why live your life in the afterlife when you still have this life to live?

Explore me with your hands, your breath, and your beingness, and see that there is nothing to fear.

A life well lived is a life that wasn't afraid to make mistakes.

Don't leave anything for the end. Use up everything that you have inside you, so when the end comes, you can laugh your way into an endless slumber knowing you gave it all you had.

ESHA ESTAR

Grief Shaman

Don't hide your fears from me. Come closer; share them with me. Let's talk about them and then go and live from that place of no fear. There you will see yourself set on fire to live life passionately.

There are many things that die constantly in your life. Observe those things, and give gratitude that you're already in relationship with me.

Love. In the end it is love. Death teaches you to open your heart to love. It is the true spiritual teacher you seek during your earthly walk.

ESHA ESTAR

Grief Shaman

There is a need for the hidden space in your heart that remains quiet to speak. Know that you don't have to wait for the deathbed conversation. Speak honestly and openly about what resides in that soft place. Let the conversation of your heart begin now.

In the end, the heart breaks free and open. It is no longer encased in the steely cage you locked it in. I urge you to talk to each other now. Do not wait for a visit from me to unburden yourself.

Awake each day being born anew. Let death wash away all the crimes of yesterday, and let the sun rise on what you can do today.

ESHA ESTAR

Grief Shaman

Some say it is morbid to talk about death. I say it is life-giving.

You have been wounded time and time again, and yet all
those wounds dissolve when death comes to your shores, and
you are left with the desire to be surrounded by love.

I wait for you to gain the courage to accept me, to see me not
as your enemy but as an ally on your evolutionary path.

Death whispers to me, "You are more than this body." I want to believe.

ESHA ESTAR

Grief Shaman

Allowing yourself to acknowledge the deaths you're experiencing daily prepares you for the inevitable. It is practice.

Make peace with all your hurts and all your pains, and leave room for love to enter in a tiny little space in your armor. There you will find the courage to surrender as the last breath approaches.

Regrets! Don't build these into your résumé. Instead, look to the joys you can interview, and then live an abundant life working for them, so the end of life comes with a life well lived.

In the end, your entire life is celebrated, so don't get caught up in doing it right. Live.

ESHA ESTAR

Grief Shaman

Death has never hidden its agenda from us; we know it will arrive one day. In that way, boundaries do not exist with death; we are free. Find that boundary-less place in your life now, and learn to live free. It is practice for death.

Death says, "I am a place where you can be free. Is there such a place where you can practice that freedom in your living life? If you can, you will experience true joy of life and death in the living life."

It is your fear that is the death of your being. Practice dying to your fears, and you will practice freedom.

Contemplate me.

ESHA ESTAR
Grief Shaman

In the East I am there, in the West I am there, in the South
I am there, in the North I am there. I am everywhere.

You cannot know life until you've experienced me in some way.

When your beloved dies, you are afraid to look me in the eyes.
Suddenly, you know your finiteness and become uncomfortable.

When your love one dies, the pain in your chest is so tight, the fear
so high for now you know that this life could in any moment end.

There is a knowing deep within your soul that this life
is temporary. This is the root of your fear.

In life there are many deaths.

ESHA ESTAR

Grief Shaman

I reach for you, and you pull away. I call your name, and you don't respond. Constantly, you refuse to recognize me in your path. I long for you to befriend me so I can set you free.

Each moment that arrives, let it wash over you like a ray of light. Let your life radiate in every moment; let the whisper of breath kiss your lips to speak love. For in too short a time, your life is gone.

There is a silence that greets you on the deathbed, where words no longer matter. It is in this place that the great spirits come to take you home. The unfinished business is finished.

Don't forget to honor the ancestors, for they come to welcome you home with love and celebration.

The seas come rushing in with the great spirits to guide you home. Their ancient language sweeps toward you. Welcome the end as it brings a brand-new beginning.

ESHA ESTAR

Grief Shaman

What you really want to say to me is "Leave me alone and fuck off." Yet what I want to say to you is "Come closer."

The more you cling, the more you die.

I am a compelling reason why you should let go of the small, petty things.

Mystery, I am mystery.

Am I not beautiful?

Spend some time with the dying, and learn how to become familiar with your mortality.

ESHA ESTAR

Grief Shaman

You are not prepared to meet me.

Don't let the phone call in the middle of the
night be the reason sleep eludes you.

I'm inevitable. Talk about me now.

I am in the breath.

In death we learn how to live. In life we learn how to die.

Each moment then is a constant
gift to behold.

ESHA ESTAR

Grief Shaman

You draw in the last breath that gurgles an entire existence
lived and exhale what is no longer yours to keep.

Death is a mystery you arrive into. You must leave
understanding at the door before you enter.

You pad yourself up with layers of untruths only to have
them unravel when you are met with your mortality.

Me talking to death: "Forgive me. I thought I was invincible."

Death rips off the old, worn-out garments that we carried
this lifetime and replaces them with something new.

Each layer of the death process is meant for us to drop our façade of
invincibility and come face-to-face with a certainty that this too shall end.

ESHA ESTAR

Grief Shaman

Don't bring your logical mind to the deathbed. Instead, enter with
that space behind your heart that is familiar with mystery.

In inviting death to teach me, I finally learned
how to grow into a mature human.

What have I seen by accepting death at my borders? I saw my fears,
mistrust, regrets, guilt, and limitations. By naming them, I found
courage, trust, forgiveness, and the freedom to be. I am free.

ESHA ESTAR
Grief Shaman

Printed in the United States
By Bookmasters